The Renewal of Baptismal Vows

by
Colin Buchanan
Vicar, St. Mark's, Gillingham, Kent
Honorary Assistant Bishop, Diocese of Rochester

gb GROVE BOOKS LIMITED
Bramcote   Nottingham   NG9 3DS

CONTENTS

FOREWORD

I was invited to contribute in 1987 to the Jubilee edition of *Studia Liturgica*, and chose to write on 'The Renewal of Baptismal Vows'. This Booklet draws upon the earlier (more sketchy) work I did in that article, and applies it more closely to the life of the Church of England.

THE COVER PICTURE

is by Peter Ashton

First Impression April 1993
ISSN 0305-3067
ISBN 1 85174 234 4

INTRODUCTION

I have written in various ways and various places in the past about baptismal issues, particularly as they relate to infant baptism, and I do not want to repeat here the same materials.[1]

But I am constantly asked, at meetings about Christian initiation (and sometimes at others), as to whether a serious individual renewal of baptismal vows—including such renewal in water, and even including such renewal with submersion in water—has any place in our liturgical patterns. Clearly such a provision must be orientated to meet identifiable pastoral needs, but to meet them with flexible materials of theological soundness and liturgical integrity. Hence I have attempted to put together here both some background about the developing pastoral need and the synodical grappling at meeting it, and also some actual practical advice. I do not think it exists elsewhere in similar compass, and that is my major excuse for writing it now.

There have been some historic ways in which the Churches have practised a renewal of baptismal vows, and some of those antecedents of the present situation I trace out in chapter 1. However, in the Church of England itself, despite the antecedents, it is likely that until the last decade or so only a few specialists advocated, let alone practised, anything that would to-day be classified as a rite for renewal of baptismal vows. It is a growth of the 1980s, prompted in part by post-Vatican II Roman Catholic uses, which have influenced liturgical revision in the Church of England, and thus brought possibilities into parish reckoning. However, there are strands of pastoral need, which had been developing independently of liturgical revision, and the new respectability of renewing baptismal vows has met these needs in a timely way.[2]

So to what needs do I refer? I am not now speaking of whole congregations corporately renewing their vows—the area in which excess

---

[1] There are currently available in print the following titles in the Grove Booklets on Ministry and Worship and the Grove Worship Series: No. 20, *A Case for Infant Baptism* (1973, (4) 1990); No. 24 (jointly with David Pawson), *Infant Baptism under Cross-Examination* (1974, (4) 1993); No. 61, *One Baptism Once* (1978, (3)1989); No. 65, *Liturgy for Initiation: The Series 3 Services* (1979); No. 91, *Adult Baptisms* (1985); No. 98, *Policies for Infant Baptism* (1987); No. 112, *Children in Communion* (1990). There are also Grove Liturgical Study no. 48, *Anglican Confirmation* (1986) and my contributions to symposia—particularly to: Colin Buchanan, Trevor Lloyd and Harold Miller (eds.) *Anglican Worship Today: Collins Illustrated Guide to the Alternative Service Book 1980* (Collins Liturgical Publications, 1980); Donald Withey (ed.) *Adult Initiation* (Alcuin/GROW Joint Liturgical Study no. 10, 1988); Colin Buchanan, Clifford Owen, Alan Wright, *Reforming Infant Baptism* (Hodder and Stoughton 1990, now remaindered and available cheap from COB); David Holeton (ed.) *Growing in Newness of Life* (Anglican Book Centre, Toronto, 1993—imported into Britain by the Canterbury Press, Norwich). There will also shortly be published my more solid book, *Infant Baptism and the Gospel* (Darton, Longman and Todd, 1993).

[2] It perhaps should be noted that there are first signs that liturgists themselves now show occasional hesitation lest the 'renewing vows' pudding has been over-egged. Christopher Walsh protested recently about the renewal of ministerial vows in the Maundy Thursday rite, and Kenneth Stevenson has shown a certain antipathy to the renewal of baptismal vows.

can trivialize the use and provoke protest. Some of the background of present-day practice lies with corporate and congregational uses, but it is not those which are centre-stage here. The issue is as to which *individual* spiritual needs a renewal of baptismal vows can helpfully minister, and it is to that issue that this booklet is addressed.

In essence, the need is for the marking, reinforcing and consolidating the experience of conversion—usually of an adult. An ever-rising tide of adults in our Churches are not 'cradle Christians' at all nowadays, but have either no Christian background from their childhood, or, if they have, they abandoned it in early life, and their present coming to faith in Christ looks and feels and is experienced as adult conversion. Such adult converts are nevertheless likely, if born in England twenty or more years ago, to have been baptized as infants. Some have even been confirmed at ten or twelve years of age. Baptists, Brethren, Pentecostalists, Independents and 'House Church' (or 'New Church') people can and do write off infant baptism, and tell converts they must be baptized as though from scratch, and not ascribe any value, let alone sacramental validity, to an infant baptism.[1] But Anglicans who value infant baptism, and practise it with a good scriptural conscience, cannot be so cavalier. Their ritual must both affirm the objective given-ness of an infant baptism standing only half-noticed at the back of an adult convert's life, and also give proper recognition and outward sustaining to the fresh new fact of conversion to Christ.

---

[1] That is not to say that these varied 'anti-pedobaptists' would never have any need for a rite for renewing baptismal vows. But they do not have to cope with the particular problem of relating adult conversion to infant baptism (for they solve that by simply eliminating infant baptism itself from the discussion); and even with 'believer's baptism' they often view baptism as a 'once-off' event with significance and high experiential value at the point where it is given, but *not* as a context-setting event within which the whole of the rest of the person's discipleship is to be lived. Any 'renewing' of the Christian commitment is therefore less likely to be conceived in baptismal terms. I actually have no knowledge of any practice of a renewal of baptismal commitment in such Churches, and thus I simply speculate in the awareness of my ignorance.

1. BAPTISM—AND THE INVOKING OF BAPTISM

What then is baptism? I shall have to answer this by mere assertion, as I have argued elsewhere about it.[1] I therefore submit the following propositiions for consideration:

1. Baptism is *the* Christian initiatory rite, leading the enquirer into the common life of the Christian church.

2. If it is appropriate to baptize infants, then it can only be done with the same theology as adult baptism.[2] In each case baptism must have the same meaning in the recipient's life, if it is to count as the same baptism at all. In particular infant baptism must include a commitment to repentance from sin, a living faith in Jesus Christ, membership of the living Christian community, and an entry upon 'the new life' (Romans 6.7).

3. Because baptism is once for all for life (which it is), the person who receives it not only undergoes the rite at a particular point in time, but also thereafter becomes by that very rite a *baptized person*, and remains so. Baptism is always 'there'—not only in the personal history but in the present personal make-up.[3]

4. Because baptism becomes a 'given' feature of a Christian person's life, it is 'there' as a basis for an appeal to living the Christian life and growing in it. The appeal does not appear to be a call to *remember the event* of being baptized. That is not strictly in view (which is a confirmatory bit of evidence that baptizing infants is in principle perfectly in line with the scriptures). My own reading of Paul in, say, Romans 6.3-6, is that he is assuming that the fulcrum of baptism is in place in all his readers' lives (again pointing towards the rightness of baptizing infants), and that he then places the lever of the word upon that fulcrum to move them forwards in their Christian lives. Whilst the emphasis is upon God's searching significance denoted in their baptism, rather than upon their own response of solemn vows, it is clear that the desired outcome, that the readers should 'walk in newness of life' (Rom. 6.4), carries baptismal obligations which are but a hairsbreadth from an overt set of vows. The only point to make here is that the vows are responsive to a recognition of God's love, though some expression of repentance and faith should normally *precede* baptism, as the formal basis for baptizing the particular candidates.[4]

It follows from the above that a proper way of viewing the Christian life is to describe it as 'living out your baptism' or 'conforming to your baptism'. The given-ness of the sacrament, and its perseverance within the life of the baptized person, mean that appeal to it can always be made in the exhorting of Christian people to holiness ('newness of life'). Whilst the

---

[1] I have discussed what is to *count* as a baptism in *One Baptism Once*, but the issue here lies in the significance of baptism.

[2] My *A Case for Infant Baptism* makes an argument for infant baptism, arguing from agreed ground about the nature of baptism in the New Testament, and thus keeping it in line with adult baptism. Obviously any invoking of the significance of a past baptism must not be suspended upon the condition 'it depends upon what sort of baptism you received'.

[3] This sense of remaining a 'baptized person' is what lay behind the medieval concept that baptism imprints a 'character' (i.e. the Greek word for a 'seal'—nothing to with personality) on the soul. This is a metaphysical way of saying that baptism once given cannot be given again; indeed it is obvious, once the concept of 'being a baptized person' has been established, that it would be otiose and misleading to take that person through that rite a second time.

[4] See chapter 2 below for a fuller discussion of the vows.

apostolic writers of the New Testament do not write treatises on baptism, they do treat the Christian life—individual and corporate alike—as lived on the basis of the given baptism. It is thus perfectly normal and regular to urge people not only to live the life of faith, but to do so *because they are baptized people*. This is the kind of invoking to be found in many of the major texts about baptism in the New Testament letters:

'Do you not know that as many of us as were baptized into Christ Jesus were baptized into his death? We were buried therefore with him by baptism into death; that, as Christ was raised from the dead by the glory of the Father, we also should walk in newness of life . . . You also should thus reckon yourselves to be dead to sin, but alive to God in Christ Jesus . . .' (Rom. 6.3-4,11)

'For it was in the one Spirit that we were all baptized into one body . . . Now the body is not one member, but many [and you are to live accordingly] . . .' (1 Cor. 12.13a,14)

'For as many of you as were baptized into Christ have put on Christ [and therefore are one in Christ, Jew and Greek, and have no need to make Greeks into Jews to be Christian] . . .' (Gal. 3.27)

'Be eager to sustain the oneness of the Spirit in the bond of peace; [for] there is one body and one Spirit . . .one Lord, one faith, one baptism . . .' (Eph. 4.3-5)

'Watch lest someone takes you captive . . . because . . . in him [Christ] you were also circumcised . . .with the circumcision of Christ, having been buried with him by baptism, in which you were also raised with him . . .' (Col. 2.8-12)

There are other similar instances. The significance of baptism, once given, is contemporary, living and effective. It is a regular, if unsystematic, point of reference for discipleship in the New Testament. The citing of it is remarkably close in significance to the modern liturgical 'renewal of baptismal vows'. Similarly, the other way round, the liturgical usage of to-day is well grounded in scriptural ways of invoking baptism.

Perhaps the major difference between most modern liturgical practices and the New Testament invoking of baptism is that the latter is drafted more in terms of God's benefits towards us (and thus his claims upon us) through baptism. Our modern practice focuses more upon our response to his love and to his claims than upon the love and claims themselves. These two emphases can each be adjusted to the other. No 'vows' must suggest human initiative towards God, let alone a kind of price we pay to belong to him; but equally, no assertions about God's claims upon us in and through baptism ought to disregard or over-ride the terms upon which we receive the gospel—personal repentance and faith.

If we take the New Testament seriously, there is great dignity, great responsibility, great gospel-centredness in being baptized. There is constant back-reference to it. There is even the injunction to be 'renewed' (as, e.g. in Rom. 12.2, or, with a different Greek verb, in Eph. 4.23). If the 'newness' which is intended to stem from baptism (see Rom. 6.4, quoted above) is to be 'renewed', then it is far from absurd to suggest not only a daily attitude of mind—a spirituality—which carries this into action in a life, but also a liturgical form—a rite—to give focal expression to it.

2. THE NATURE OF VOWS IN INFANT BAPTISM

There is one further preamble to take aboard before we come to rites for renewing baptismal vows. It consists simply of an enquiry as to whether one baptized as an infant actually *has* any baptismal vows to renew. There has been a strong sentiment over recent years which has viewed the notion of godparents and/or parents taking or making vows 'on behalf of' a child as very unreal, and possibly immoral. Would it not be better for the parents simply to undertake to give the child a Christian upbringing?

There is much point in having parents give their own undertakings about the child's upbringing. The ASB rite includes the opening question:
    Children . . . are baptized on the understanding that they are brought up as Christians within the family of the Church . . .

    Parents and godparents, the *children* whom you have brought for baptism depend chiefly on for the help and encouragement they need. Are you willing to give it to *them* by your prayers, by your example, and by your teaching? (ASB, page 243)

So parents' statements about themselves and about their intentions in relation to the children have their place. They initially—even formally—qualify the children to *be* candidates at all.[1] But these statements are not of themselves the baptismal vows. For these we go back to the early church practice, revived for the Church of England in the ASB, of having adults and infants baptized *together*.[2] The earliest instance of which we have evidence is in Hippolytus' *Apostolic Tradition*, dated around 215 AD. There he says:
    'As for those who cannot speak for themselves, their parents or someone from their family shall speak for them.'
Then the rite simply continues in a form which is apparently identical for adults and infants. Certainly that is how the rite developed in the West. No-one ever wrote a service specifically designed for infants—rather it continued, even with relics of a catechumenate, as a variant on a standard (adult) rite. The godparents answered the questions 'in the name' of the child, and the undertakings were understood to belong to the infant.

The Reformers in turn inherited this pattern of rites for infant baptism: in sixteenth century Europe the baptism of adults had long since ceased, and the only issue as between different rites was whether infants should or could be baptized at home in emergency (emergencies relating to infant mortality were very frequent at the time)—or whether all baptisms should be conducted in church. In the Church of England they also retained the proxy form of vows, in which the godparents were addressed as though

---

[1] This is of course the upshot of a biblical enquiry into whether there is any case for infant baptism anyway, and is itself the basis for all consideration of policies to identify proper candidates for infant baptism.
[2] See the first rite in the ASB, pages 225-235.

they *were* the child, on exactly the same basis as Hippolytus had ordered in the third century:

Dost thou forsake the devil and all his works?

What dost thou desire?

Wilt thou be baptized?[1]

The catechism (which was part of the confirmation service in 1549 and 1552) asked the candidate about his or her baptism:
What did your godfathers and godmothers then for you?

And the answer was:
They did promise and vow three things in my name . . .

And the follow-up was
Dost thou not think thou art bound to believe and do as they have promised for thee?

The obedient candidate then found himself or herself responding:
Yes verily.

So the proxy expression of vows, which, as vows, *truly belonged to the candidate* (rather than to the parent or godparent), was well entrenched in the BCP. It fell into some disrepute in the 1960s, and the Series 2 rite was ambiguous on the point. In Series 3 (1979) and the ASB rite, the parents and godparents (now dubbed 'sponsors') are required to answer 'both for yourselves and for this child'. So there is no escape into ambiguity now.[2] And whereas, for pastoral (or disciplinary) reasons the average clergyman of the last thirty years has been keen to have sponsors to recognize that they are making statements about their *own* repentance and faith, liturgical purists and those who are dealing with people trying to make sense of their own previous infant baptism, will want to stress that the vows belong primarily to the *candidate*. It is actually logically very odd if one person (say a parent) promises lifelong obedience to Christ, *and another different person is baptized*! We would look to be in danger of having two baptisms—one with obligations to walk in newness of life, and one without.

Of course the meaning of baptism is not solely wrapped up in the liturgical form used at the administration of the sacrament. So, even if there were

[1] This style of questions is identical in 1549 and 1552 (though the wording of them varies slightly from one to the other). Amusingly, however, the rationale in the opening rubric shifts about:
Then shall the priest demand of the child . . . these questions following; first naming the child, and saying: (1549)
Then shall the priest demand of the Godfathers and Godmothers these questions following. (1552)
In 1662 the form of the question is:
Dost thou, in the name of this child, . . .?
[2] For a fuller discussion of this point, see my *Liturgy for Initiation: The Series 3 Services* (Grove Booklet on Ministry and Worship no. 65, 1979), and my forthcoming book, *Infant Baptism and the Gospel* (Darton, Longman and Todd, 1993).

no vows, it is in fact still proper to examine the meaning of baptism, especially infant baptism, and see the implications of it, even if they were not spelled out in the rite at the time it was given.[1] If it was Christian baptism at all, then the significance was implicit within it, even if not spelled out. That would certainly have to be reckoned as part of people being baptized people.

Our conclusion is, therefore, that, if there is a case for baptizing infants at all, then it is a case for a full New Testament baptism (not just a pale variant on it), and that means that, whether explicitly or implicitly, the very giving of the baptism is a process of binding upon the recipient the Christian obligation to live a holy life. The recipient may or may not at that or any later stage acknowledge the claims of Christ upon her or him—that will vary. But the objectivity of that claim, and the formal statement in baptism (whether articulated or not) that discipleship to Christ follows from that point—those should be undisputed.

I submit therefore not only that infant baptism is true Christian baptism, but that in that baptism there is asserted a claim upon the candidate to live and grow as a Christian disciple, and in the receiving of the baptism there is a formal acknowledgement of that claim.

None of that means that anything automatic follows from the giving of infant baptism or the getting it ritually correct. It is the task of other writings to press the case for a credible and principled administration of infant baptism in a post-Christian society.[2] But even if such a practice came about, it would still leave millions of people in this country, let alone tens of millions elsewhere, who had received an indiscriminately ministered, wholly valid, infant baptism, and had never lived in the light of that baptism since. It is when those people come to adult faith that the issue of 'Renewal of Baptismal Vows' most frequently comes to the fore.

[1] Quite apart from those denominations which may give infant baptism without the candidate making vows, the practice of emergency baptism in the Church of England (see ASB, pages 280-281) can have the same effect. The theory (rubric 110) is that the baptized person, child or adult, now recovered from the sickbed and the brink of death, is brought to church and, cosmetically, catches up with the vows—but of course that does not always happen.

[2] See my *Policies for Infant Baptism* (Grove Worship Booklet 98, 1987), or the forthcoming *Infant Baptism and the Gospel, op. cit.*, or the sources cited in chapter 3 of that book. For a statement of the official stance of the Church of England see my *Infant Baptism in the Church of England: A Guide to the Official Position of the Church in its Formularies* (Grove Books, 1992). For information on the Movement for the Reform of Infant Baptism (MORIB) write to the Rev. Clifford Owen, the Rectory, Clifton-on-Teme, Worcs.

3. SOME HISTORICAL BACKGROUND AND DEVELOPMENTS

If we find ourselves to-day with a pastoral need for a rite for a renewal of baptismal vows, it may be helpful to stand back a little and look at historical precedents.

Arguably the earliest precedents are in rites for restoration of the lapsed, apostate or excommunicate. It is possible that the first record of this is in 2 Corinthians 2.5-8. In the succeeding centuries there was a great concern for the purity of the church's life and witness, and corresponding unwillingness to restore the lapsed. But it is likely that the developed Western doctrine of Penance itself had these roots, the presbyter taking upon himself the power to deal privately with that which had previously been public. Baptism may not have been strongly in view in the administration of medieval penance, but the theologians could refer to it as the 'second plank'—i.e. the stand-by after people had breached the terms of the 'first plank': baptism.

There is a closer precedent in reformed rites of confirmation. In the pre-Reformation time, although confirmation would not normally have been given to infants, yet the rite was based on the assumption that they were infants.[1] Consequently the origins of the rite within a complex initiation rite, even as given to infants, were still discernible. In practice, in the Middle Ages children had to make their overt response to their earlier baptism by reciting Paternoster and Ave Maria at first confession in preparation for first communion, and confirmation was a much more random rite, which might come at any point in childhood—or none.[2] However, as it was normally given from seven upwards, it was waiting for the Reformers to give a more standardized pastoral significance to it. This they did by treating the rite as a certificate of catechetical testing, and, as we have seen, the new catechism of Cranmer was built into the confirmation service in 1549 and 1552, and the back-reference from confirmation to baptism was as is quoted above.[3] It was only in 1662 that the catechism was divided from the confirmation rite, and so the question of what response the candidates should make within the confirmation rite arose. In the event it was resolved with this question from the bishop:

> Do ye here, in the presence of God, and of this Congregation, renew the solemn promise and vow that was made in your name at your Baptism: ratifying and confirming the same in your own persons, and acknowledging yourselves bound to believe and to do all those things which your Godfathers and Godmothers then undertook for you?

> *Ans:* I do.

---

[1] The delay occurred because infants were baptized as quickly after birth as possible (lest they die unbaptized), but they could not be confirmed till a bishop appeared. The difficulties of travel and other calls (including old age) upon bishops meant that large numbers of children never got confirmed.

[2] What cannot be obtained is rationalized in practice as not actually needed. So the Middle Ages had a fairly low view of confirmation—which is lamented by Dix and co., but actually helped the Reformers establish the sufficiency of baptism alone for sacramental initiation.

[3] See page 8 above. For fuller detail of the Reformation era, see my *Anglican Confirmation* (Grove Liturgical Study 48, 1986) pp.19-25. Curiously, it was some erroneous early church history by John Calvin which heled fix the post-Reformation character of confirmation (see *Anglican Confirmation*, p.19).

This question and answer may well have been the first to put the verb 'renew' into liturgy in this connection. The phrase 'in your own persons' also establishes that, whatever identity of godparents and candidate can be assumed at the actual infant baptism, everybody knows that the infant has not overtly professed anything as from himself or herself, and the addition of this personal profession is desirable.[1] Later versions have taken up the baptismal vows in more detail, and have thus spelled out separate vows at confirmation; but the principle has remained the same. And latter-day discussion would detach the incidental feature of admission to communion from confirmation of teenagers and twelve-year-olds, and thus major more heavily upon the mature ratification of the baptismal vows, which had been articulated by proxy in infant baptism.

Confirmation has been once for all for life, and has traditionally involved selected candidates only at the particular point in life where they have been ready (after preparation) for that renewal. However, there are precedents for a more corporate pattern of renewal. From a wholly different strand of history comes the Methodist Covenant Service. It was begun by John Wesley in 1755 and was used at high seasons, as, e.g. at the beginning of Conference or at other times of rededication. It looks as though it was used at New Year from at least 1772. Wesley himself referred to it as 'renewing our Covenant with God'—a pattern which, in the thought-forms of Wesley, was a re-binding of ourselves to God. This rite lacked any baptismal back-reference in Wesley's thought, probably because he was himself unwilling to see baptism as the foundation of the church's life, and knew that he was handling new spiritual life of a sort that sprang from true individual conversion and not universal baptism. Modern rites in both British Methodism and the Church of South India include reference to 'being born into the family of God, and made members of the body of Christ', and yet still do not mention baptism. It is the concept of renewing which comes over strongly.

On the other hand, the Roman Catholic practice of sprinkling holy water has usually had some back-reference to baptism, even if it has often been implicit. When the Easter Vigil rite was revised in 1951, for the first time there was an overt renewal of the congregation's baptismal vows, and it was accompanied by this sprinkling—the asperges. It was intended, if possible, to accompany actual baptisms, with the same water being used. And the practice has spread into all kinds of other Christian Churches. In particular, the Church of England, which first raised the possibility in the

---

[1] This is reinforced in other ways: the title of the rite is 'The Order of Confirmation, or the Laying on of Hands upon those that are Baptized and come to Years of Discretion'; and in the Preface the bishop (or another minister) reads what was a rubric in 1552, that
'. . . children being now come to the years of discretion, and having learned what their Godfathers and Godmothers promised for them in Baptism, they may themselves, *with their own mouth and consent,* openly before the Church, ratify and confirm the same; and also promise, that by the grace of God they will evermore endeavour themselves faithfully to observe such things, as they *by their own confession have assented unto.'*
The italics here are mine. Whilst there may be some dispute as to whether any sacramental import remained in the 1552 and 1662 rites for confirmation, the ratifying of (infant) baptismal vows is not in question. It was central.

ASB, now has full semi-official texts of this sort in *Lent, Holy Week, Easter*.[1] These provide for a renewal of the congregation's baptismal vows immediately following the actual baptisms and/or confirmations.[2] A further development has now come in *Promise of His Glory*, where Epiphany includes a commemoration of the Lord's baptism by John, and opportunity is taken for 'The Renewal of the Covenant'.[3] This is modelled upon the Methodist Covenant Service, and, because it falls on 6 January or the Sunday after, it nearly or actually coincides with the Methodist use of their Covenant Service. However, there is one obvious difference—here in *Promise* the 'renewal' relates to the significance of baptism itself, and the 'turning to Christ' is itself rooted in baptism. That seems sheer gain.

There are also signs from around the world of a more individual provision arising. This involves rites for a variety of occasions. Thus in the Episcopal Church of the USA the confirmation service in the 1979 Prayer Book includes provision for those being 'received into this Communion' and those 'reaffirming their baptismal vows'. Both these categories of candidates renew their 'baptismal covenant' along with the confirmation candidates, but have a different form of words used at the laying on of hands:
(for Reception) *N.*, we recognize you as a member of the one holy catholic and apostolic Church, and we receive you into the fellowship of this Communion. God, the Father, Son, and Holy Spirit, bless, preserve, and keep you. **Amen.**

(for Reaffirmation)
N., may the Holy Spirit, who has begun a good work in you direct and uphold you in the service of Christ and his kingdom. **Amen.**[4]

The Canadian *Book of Alternative Services* (1985) reproduces the American texts for the three categories of renewal of vows within the confirmation provision.[5] However, the Book also has an interesting variant on the American pattern, in that it provides for the reconciliation of a penitent by grouping it in the Book in juxtaposition with baptism, which the American Book does not. It includes within the normal form a question drawn from the American Book: 'Do you turn again to Christ?' The reply is 'I turn to Christ'.[6] So overall there is a slightly stronger echo of baptism in this than in the American texts.[7]

[1] See ASB, pages 275-278, where the opening Notes mention Easter (in line with the Roman Catholic practice), and New Year (in line with the Methodist Covenant Service). *Lent, Holy Week, Easter* (1986) is 'Commended by the House of Bishops', and the relevant part of the Easter liturgy is on pages 234-5. The rite makes no provision for a form of 'blessing the water' for the asperges on occasions when there is no actual baptism.
[2] My own experience is that, if adults are being plunged—i.e. submerged—in baptism, then they need up to 15 minutes to get dry and changed, and it is good sense to renew the congregation's baptismal vows during those 15 minutes, and not delay that item until after the confirmation.
[3] *The Promise of His Glory* (1991) is also 'commended by the House of Bishops'; 'The Renewal of the Covenant' is on pages 218-222.
[4] The Book of Common Prayer (1979) pp.418-419. It is also interesting that, immediately following the confirmation rite which contains these options, the Book contains 'A Form of Commitment to Christian Service' (pp.420-421). This directs by rubric that a 'reaffirmation of baptismal promises' should be included within the act of commitment.
[5] See *BAS* pages 625-629.
[6] See *BAS* page 168, and cf. the American BCP, page 450.
[7] See the discussion earlier on this page.

The Church of the Province of Southern Africa authorized *An Anglican Prayer Book* in 1989. This contains an admission of baptized communicants from other Churches (which has similarities to confirmation, but takes geunine account of the different situation, including the words at the laying on of hands); it also contains 'Renewal of Baptismal Promises' which suggests both 'free and spontaneous prayer' and the opportunity for testimony. It does not include any special ceremony, and is like a development of the ASB provision—i.e. something largely intended for the whole congregation at once (though that testimony possibility might refer to simply a small or self-selecting group).[1]

In *A New Zealand Prayer Book* (1989) the rite is included within the baptismal provision, and the total contents are labelled *'The Liturgy of Baptism and The Laying on of Hands for Confirmation and Renewal'*. The profession of faith is the same for those newly baptized and those reaffirming their faith, and there is a further interrogation about commitment to service. There is then a dual provision for the laying on of hands— candidates may be confirmed or may receive 'renewal'. In the latter case the laying on of hands has the following prayer accompanying it:

Creator Spirit,
rekindle in *N* your gifts of grace,
renew *her/his* life in Christ
and bring to completion
all that your calling has begun.
Amen.

The texts take a little unravelling (partly because of complexities in the baptismal part), but the intention is clear.[2]

There is similar provision in the recent ecumenical rites produced in Britain as *Confirmaton and Re-affirmation of Baptismal Faith*.[3] There the laying on of hands is practised at 'Re-affirmation' but no other ceremony.

The general thrust of these other rites is to make the texts more flexible and open in respect of the candidates, and to give opportunity for the individual to be identified separately according to his or her needs. There is also a possibility that laying on of hands may carry various titles, and may cease to be once-for-all-for-life in a well-advertised unique rite called 'confirmation'.[4] There is, however, no mention of using water at the reaf-

---

[1] *An Anglican Prayer Book* (1989), pp.399-404.
[2] *A New Zealand Prayer Book* (1989), pp.388-393.
[3] Compiled by the Joint Liturgical Group and published by the Canterbury Press, Norwich, 1992.
[4] This is almost a commonplace of recent discussion. However, despite its meretricious appeal, it needs careful handling: as long as there is a requirement anywhere in a Church's rules for people to be confirmed to qualify for certain roles (membership of Synods or Church Councils, being godparents, being candidates for ordination, etc. there must remain one identifiable rite which is confirmation. Proposals to change the uniqueness of the rite are fine in themselves (there is no particular scriptural basis for it), but they have to be comprehensive across the board and wrap in all the rules as well, or they are self-defeating.

firmation of baptismal vows.[1] The nearest that might be found is the 1988 Lambeth reference to 'appropriate meaningful ceremonies'—but even there it was deemed imexpedient to make direct reference to water.[2]

Finally, we come to the Fourth International Anglican Liturgical Consultation at Toronto in 1991. Now water gets a mention, though even there a defensiveness about ceremonies tends to neutralize most of what is written.[3] Indeed inspection of the text shows that no sooner has it said that a request for 'immersion' must be taken seriously than it itself dismisses it summarily! But at least water—and the needs and requests of individuals—are getting on the agenda.

---

[1] That does not, of course, mean that such uses were never found; and I have vivid recollections of David Penman in 1981 (when he was vicar of All Saints, Palmerston North in New Zealand—before he became first a suffragan bishop, then the metropolitan, in Melbourne) telling me how he submerged candidates at a public renewal of their baptismal vows, taking great trouble to ensure that they themselves understood what they were doing.

[2] *The Truth Shall Make You Free: The Lambeth Conference 1988* (ACC, 1989) p.72.

[3] '... the requests of those looking for both immersion in water and for the laying on of hands to mark a significant experience of the Spirit must be taken seriously. For them, a lesser ceremony will not do, and a more specific rite, which may include both the laying on of hands and the use of water, as well as provision for public catechesis or testimony, should be provided. We believe that care should be taken not to deny the baptism that has already taken place in the person's life, or the mode of that baptism by affusion.[1] No province should adopt a form of this kind until it is satisfied that neither those involved nor others who are aware of it will confuse it with baptism.

To avoid confusion with baptism we urge that the following be noted in the preparation of any rite for local use:
—words which define what is happening should be said by the whole congregation;
—words should be used to affirm clearly the baptism which has already taken place in the person's life;
—water may be used by a minister in a manner which is not suggestive of baptism, e.g. sprinkling a number of people at once, but not individually;
—the sign of the cross in water or oil may be made by the persons themselves or by sponsors.
(The Toronto Statement 'Walk in Newness of Life' paras 20-21, to be found in Grove Worship Series no. 118, David Holeton (ed.) *Christian Initiation in the Anglican Communion* (Grove Books, 1991) p.18; or in David Holeton (ed.) *Growing in Newness of Life* (ABC, Toronto, 1993) pp.246-7.)

[1] Methods of baptism vary from submersion (the water completely (the candidate kneels or stands in water which is also poured over the head), to affusion (water poured over the head). [See Appendix 1 here—COB]

4. THE CHURCH OF ENGLAND

The 1980s have seen a growing interest in the Church of England in rituals for renewing baptismal vows. I have given brief mention above to the corporate renewal.[1] But the major interest has lain, and does lie, in the personal and individual renewal—possibly in and with the use of water. Indeed the whole 'experiential' emphasis of the Charismatic Movement in the Church of England has in the last twenty years increased pressures against infant baptism—and this in turn has meant that those who needed to defend infant baptism had to look at the experiential side of a rite for renewal of baptismal vows. I suspect that an article published in the (now defunct) *Theological Renewal* in 1978, reporting an officially approved rite of the Presbyterian Church of New Zealand, quickened the interest. Certainly I have heard constant reference to this article over the last fifteen years. For convenience I reproduce it entire below as Appendix 2.[2]

Let there be no mistake. There exists in the life of any church which baptizes infants a restiveness amongst adult converts on this very point. Such people, if they are told forcefully that they have been baptized—truly and validly baptized—in infancy, often have a sense of hurt that they have been deprived of a crucial milestone in their coming to faith. Others will tell them that their infant baptism was no baptism, and that, now they are converted, they need to go to some other church or assembly where they can now be 'properly' baptized. (The Church of England's standard answer has been that such people should now be confirmed; but (a) sometimes they already have been, and (b) even if not, the external pressure towards a 'second baptism' may still be very strong; and it is often compounded internally by the emotional 'pull' of a rite of such total breaking with the past, and possibly also with a sense of God's call or guidance.[3])

The more I have reflected on this and counselled actual persons in the tension that this creates, the more sure I have become that submersion is both possible and desirable for some in this category.[4] Anyone, of course, who denies that infant baptism *is* Christian baptism under any circumstances cannot be helped by Anglicans. Such people are *bound* either to live in some misery in one of our congregations, or to leave and go to an anti-pedobaptist denomination.[5] But there is a bracket of persons who, longing for both the actual experience and the symbolism of a total swamping in line with baptism, are nevertheless ready to acknowledge that infant baptism *is* baptism (even if undesirable), that therefore they themselves *are* baptized, and that therefore the rite they wish to undergo

[1] See page 3 above.
[2] See page 22 below.
[3] It should be recognized that the overseas variants on confirmation, such as are described in chapter 3 above, will not necessarily help, when it is the baptismal water which exercises the pull.
[4] For the term 'submersion' see Appendix 1 on page 21 below.
[5] It has to be acknowledged that there are many people in Anglican congregations—yes, and Anglican Theological Colleges—who have had such a 'second baptism'. In my *One Baptism Once* I suggest a (provocative) form for renouncing a 'second' baptism.

will not be baptism nor be interpreted by them or others as baptism—for all that it has strong baptismal echoes.[1]

For a theological rationale, there are two lines of thought which intersect to justify the practice. One is that, in the revived tradition of the Easter Vigil, baptismal water is sprinkled or thrown upon a congregation in renewal of their baptismal vows. No-one thinks such use of the water calls in question their previous and existent baptism—the whole approach to it, and the text of renewing vows in particular, show that it is not baptism. So the first line of thought is that it is least arguable that, if water is poured from a font in baptism upon the candidates, and yet that same font can provide water for renewal of baptismal vows with asperging; then, by parity of reasoning, water which is used for submersing candidates for baptism can then be used again to submerge candidates to have their baptismal vows renewed.[1] The safeguards will lie in the texts and context, not in the avoidance of water or of submersion.[2]

The other line of thought goes as follows: we believe infant baptism to be full and complete baptism insofar as its sacramental character is concerned—yet we acknowledge that the infant has not professed faith in Christ with her or his own mouth, and so it is entirely appropriate to add that personal profession at a later date (indeed, in accordance with the whole theme of this Booklet, to add it, if appropriate, more than once). Yet such addition does not call in doubt the sufficiency of the original baptism as baptism. So, by parity of reasoning, it is appropriate to add to the initial pouring of water on an infant a later swamping or submerging, thus giving at that point the experience which the infant either missed altogether at baptism or at most received so unreflectively that its experiential value could not be conserved.

The two lines of thought duly intersect at the point where it is not only legitimate but also pastorally sensible to offer the rite.

So far, so good; however there is again some immediate background to fit in. The House of Bishops discussed in October 1987 a memorandum by

[1] On one occasion in my Birmingham days I was rung up by the diocesan bishop of another diocese not a hundred miles away. He had an incumbent who had come into renewal, perhaps even conversion, since ordination! The man was near to going off for 'baptism' somewhere, a step which would, presumably, have vitiated, if not actually ended, his incumbency. The bishop referred the man to me; I saw him; he stood precisely in the position outlined above; he accepted that he was already baptized; and he came, with a churchwarden who alone in his parish knew the situation, and joined in another parish's rites in Birmingham, being simply introduced by his Christian name. He thus renewed his baptismal vows with a submersion; he retained his ministry; and his paths and mine occasionally cross to this day.
[2] There are, of course, those who want to argue that initial baptism should not be conducted by submersion, or at least that the desire for it is superstitious and historically ill-founded. There are hints of this in the House of Bishops' resolutions quoted on page 17 opposite. Some of the reply I made to this is to be found in Appendix 3 on page 26
[3] Of course avoiding water and avoiding submersion in water *will* prevent any confusion with baptism itself. Similarly living all one's life lying in bed wrapped in a heated blanket in a warm room will avoid all risks of catching cold—but in each case there *are* other less drastic ways of cramping good instincts—avoiding risks.

the Bishop of Guildford. As a result, the House of Bishops agreed:

(a) To consult with the Council for the Care of Churches and Chancellors to ensure that wherever there is to be a font which provides for baptism by immersion or submersion, it should be readily usable for baptism by affusion.

(b) To encourage bishops at baptisms and confirmations to make the most of the symbolism, especially ensuring a plentiful use of water and the close inter-relation-ship of vows and the threefold baptism; and to encourage clergy to follow such practice in their baptisms.

(c) (i) To ask the Liturgical Commission to consider again the renewal of baptismal vows, and perhaps to provide a more significant and dramatic rite than that provided in the ASB.

(ii) The Commission might also consider some rite for the restoration of the lapsed.

(iii) Meanwhile it may be appropriate not to encourage or countenance some unofficial practices which appear to be a renewal of *baptism*.

(d) To remind clergy and lay people that the earliest Christian practice was baptism by immersion, rather than by submersion, which appears to be the preferred option to-day.[1]

I had a suspicion when I read these minutes (I was not then on the House of Bishops) that I was actually myself in view as an erring practitioner in (c) (iii) in these findings.[2] I responded vigorously in *News of Liturgy* at the time, and print that response as Appendix 3 here.[3]

Unofficial practices naturally continued, with the more discerning both guarding their practice on the one hand, and insisting therefore that nothing of this sort could be confused with baptism on the other. I have myself had an almost continuous flow of enquiries and have advised on texts and safeguards widely. I have also been privileged at intervals to continue the practice myself.

Meanwhile the Liturgical Commission went to work in response to the House of Bishops' direction. Two members produced a short document which came to the debates of the House of Bishops in January 1991, and was then published and made available for the General Synod debates on initiation issues in July 1991.[4] The two authors outline what they call 'Three Routes to Christian Faith and Practice':

1. Infant baptism, leading to confirmation and communion.[5]

[1] I have discussed the terminology for application of water in baptism or in renewal of baptismal vows briefly in Appendix 1 on page 23 below.

[2] I had first submerged an adult for renewal of baptismal vows earlier that year, and had referred to it in public. I had also printed a text in Grove Worship Series no. 91 *Adult Baptisms* (1985) which included '. . .I dip you . . .in renewal of that baptism' (*op. cit.* p.24)— a text I altered to that on page . . . below after I read the House of Bishops' minutes.

[3] See Appendix 3 on page 23 below.

[4] *Christian Initiation and its Relation to Some Pastoral Offices: A Paper prepared on behalf of the Liturgical Commission by Kenneth Stevenson and David Stancliffe* (GS Misc 366) (Church House Bookshop, July 1991).

[5] At this point the authors greatly confused the issue, as they handled the 'communion before confirmation' issue (which was *the* matter of debate) as a variant on their 'Route One' ('because Confirmation remains integral to it'). It is in fact an overwhelmingly obviously different *route*—whereas their 'Route Two' (which itself still seems to have confirmation as 'integral') is simply 'Route One' compressed, and it is that which should have been listed as a minor variant on 'Route One'.

2. Baptism, confirmation and communion all in an integrated whole.

3. Their 'third route' is not in fact an alternative route, but a *subsequent*—and therefore hardly initiatory—one. For this they write about *'staged rites'*, but the three different groups of people who emerge and require 'an adapted form of Christian initiation . . . in order to ritualize reality' have all already got a secure baptismal background, and it is either slight variants on existing confirmation which are in view or a rite for reaffirmation of baptismal vows, or for reconciliation. These provisions can hardly be called a separate 'route' to or through initiation, and the treating them as 'Route Three'—after muddling the first two—adds confusion to disorder.

However, we should note here what is said about re-affirmation in this document. The authors write:
'. . . there would be a form of service resembling Confirmation, at which chrism could be used with the laying on of hands, or sprinkled water after it. There might be regulations under which the presidency of this rite could be delegated to presbyters (priests), but it should be clear it is an essentially episcopal rite. Care should be taken that such renewals do not happen more than (normally) once in a person's life, and after due preparation.'[1]

The House of Bishops took a package of motions to the General Synod in July 1991—the most notable of which were a strong hint that confirmation could be administered 'at an early age', and that existing practices of 'communion before confirmation' should be discontinued. They also proposed:
'That this Synod ask the Liturgical Commission to prepare a series of rites described as Route Three in GS Misc 366 for the renewal of baptismal vows, for the reception of members of another Church, and for reconciliation and healing.'

At the July Synod a cross-wind blew from the Bishop of Chester. He had accepted the notion of confirmation at around seven years of age, but was concerned about what should come later. He invoked the 'Reardon Report'.[2] On this basis he therefore proposed—and carried—the insertion of a further provision:
'That this Synod ask the Liturgical Commission to prepare a rite of Adult Commitment as stated in paragraph 134 of GS Misc 365.'

I suspect that (GS 365 notwithstanding) this motion muddled counsel. If the Bishop of Chester's basis for it is accepted, then confirmation would

---

[1] *op. cit.*, p.7. Note again how cautious the two are about the *amount* of water . . .
[2] This was the main background document to the July 1991 debate in Synod: *Christian Initiation—A Policy for the Church of England: A Discussion Paper* by Canon Martin Reardon (GS Misc 365) (Church House Publishing, 1991). Martin Reardon does discuss the reaffirming of baptismal vows, and is hesitatingly encouraging about the use of water (he says we need 'a re-affirmation . . . which will satisfy the emotional needs of those who might otherwise ask for "re-baptism".' (p.45)), without being very keen on 'total immersion'.

be administered at seven (though nowadays the seven-year-olds would be outnumbered by adults at the actual rite), and one's standing as a confirmed person would not be adequate for adult participation in the life of the church (e.g. as a PCC member or a godparent) if it were clear that the confirmation had been received at seven—in that case 'commitment' would have to be certified also. Yet it is difficult to see how this rite would differ from adult confirmation, and, if so, a simple admission of children to communion without a rite other than baptism, followed by adult ratification of baptismal vows in confirmation would meet the case, without our inventing extra rites . . . If anything is needed for those already confirmed (irrespective of the age at which they received confirmation), the kind of re-affirmation for which I plead here (or a possible outcome of the 'Route Three' work by the Liturgical Commission) would suffice.[1]

At the time of writing, despite the suspicion that some draft texts already existed when the Stevenson/Stancliffe document first came to the House of Bishops over two years ago, there is no record of the Commission sending any drafting to the House for either 'commendation' or introduction into Synod for authorization.

[1] There is a further slight puzzle in the Bishop of Chester's insertion: that is that, although his own position was clear in his speech, the General Synod approved his proposal, not his speech, and the proposal might mean one of several things. I would think the Commission is puzzled . . .

5. LITURGICAL PROVISION

Let it be that we have taken aboard the warnings about 're-affirmations', that they must not be confused with baptism *ab initio*; let it be that we have also taken aboard the category of pastoral needs which can best be met by a submersion of the already baptized; how is that submersion to be done in a way that avoids the dreaded confusion? For it is not the fact of submersion that of itself produces ambiguity or gives rise to the wrong interpretation—it is the way in which the event is conducted. The possibility of misinterpretation must be excluded both formally (by set liturgical forms) and informally (by ensuring that accurate descriptions alone are afoot after the event). I suggest (on the basis of various experience) a complete programme, whilst gladly acknowledging that this is not the only way the submersion and the safeguards can both be put in place together.[1]

Curiously the distinguishing from baptism *ab initio* is most easily achieved when there are actual baptisms as well as renewals to occur. For then there are, throughout the rite, *two* categories of candidates in view, sitting or standing in different places, and responding with different words—and that makes the point very well. It is on such presuppositions that I now set out the kind of liturgical programme I have followed. It is a programme which, for obvious reasons, runs close to the liturgical material for baptisms and confirmations in the ASB.[2]

1. Preparation
Quite apart from normal adult catechetical processes (which may be similar to those for adult baptism or confirmation candidates), the candidate must be ready to acknowledge the reality of the infant (or other) baptism already received, and that should be on record, preferably signed by the candidate (which can be achieved by the use of a simple form of application), well before the liturgical event.

2. Testimony
Whilst it may not be appropriate in every case, it may be appropriate to have candidates describe their personal pilgrimage (including mention of their baptism) within the rite.[3]

---

[1] My own diocesan very understandably likes to see proposed texts in advance so as to assure himself about the safeguards, and on occasion has asked me to vet texts from a different parish which has been in touch with him. The texts and practices I describe here have been used with his goodwill.

[2] There might well be totally different approaches, and the provision by the Presbyterian Church of New Zealand, set out as Appendix 2 on page 24 below, bears little resemblance to my suggestions here.

[3] If there is any difficulty (from a time or articulation point of view), I have found that binding a testimony from all candidates into the liturgical programme booklet for the occasion can achieve the same effect. The 1988 Lambeth Conference 'Mission and Ministry' Section reported 'We also recommend in a baptism and confirmation context . . .that there is great effectiveness in "a personal word of testimony", and we suggest provision for this in the rites . . .' (*The Truth Shall Make you Free: The Lambeth Conference 1988* (ACC, 1989) p.72). Quite apart from the 'safeguarding' factor, such 'renewing' persons very often have a good story of God's grace to tell.

3. Preaching
It is not only possible, but also desirable and often instinctive to point out that there are two groups of people who are going to be submerged—that they are sitting separately, and are being submerged at different points in the rite and for different purposes.

4. Candidates' Acknowledgment
The introduction of the candidates (whether by formal presentation or not) can well include the question 'Have you been baptized or not?'. Actual baptismal candidates, when asked, answer 'no': confirmation and 'renewal' candidates answer 'yes'.[1] They thus preclude any suspicion that they themselves are entertaining reservations.[2]

5. Interrogation
Here is my text:
> You, . . ., come for baptism. Then you must now affirm your allegiance to Christ and your rejection of all that is evil.

> You, . . ., come to renew your baptismal vows in the waters of baptism, and you . . . come to be confirmed. Then you must now with your own mouth and from your own heart declare your allegiance to Christ and your rejection of all that is evil.

(The 'Decision' questions follow for all candidates together. The signing with the sign of the cross and prayer against the powers of darkness at the end of the interrogation are only used for baptism candidates.)

6. Prayer over the Water
The usual prayer from the baptism service is first used. The baptismal candidates make their baptismal profession of faith, and are duly baptized, receive the sign of the cross and candles (where appropriate), and are given 'The Welcome'.

Then those renewing their vows (again, whether in confirmation or in re-affirmation with submersion) come to edge of the water and this prayer is used:
> Heavenly Father, grant that, as by water we are baptized into the body of Christ, so grant that by this same water . . . may be stirred in living the baptismal life, and in walking in the light of their baptismal vows. Through Jesus Christ our Lord, who died for us and rose again in the new life. **Amen**.

They then make their affirmations of faith, with confirmation candidates at the edge of the water, and 'submersion' candidates possibly, though not necessarily, standing on a step with feet already in the water.

[1] I believe I owe this point to a 'leak' from a Liturgical Commission member: honour where honour is due.

[2] In this section I mention confirmation candidates, as it has usually been in the context of confirmations (and in my capacity as a bishop) that I have mostly conducted such services. But it is easily possible to eliminate the confirmation candidates from the textual provision in this and the following sections. (It is also possible to *include* confirmation candidates in the submersion programme, as they may themselves also wish to have the swamping experience.)

7. Formula at Submersion

Baptisms, of course, are usually conducted with the formula '*N*., I baptize you in the name of the Father and of the Son and of the Holy Spirit'. For the submersion for renewal of vows I use:

N, as you have been baptized in the name of the Father and of the Son and of the Holy Spirit, so now, in commemoration of that baptism, and in renewal of its meaning to you, I dip you in this water in the name of the Father, and of the Son, and of the Holy Spirit. **Amen.**

As with baptism itself, I submerge three times (though this is not obligatory), and do so in the citing of name of the Trinity in the last lines of the formula.

If a candle is to be given, then it is lit by those baptized slightly earlier and passed to the 'renewing' candidates, with these words:

This is to show that you have renewed your walk in the light.

All: **Shine as lights in the world to the glory of God the Father.**

There is of course no 'Welcome', though there may be applause.

8. Certification

Each candidate receives a written and signed statement that he or she, acknowledging his or her already existent baptism, had renewed the baptismal vows with a submersion in commemoration of the original baptism and in renewal of its meaning; and that a record of this has been put in the parish magazine and clipped into the baptismal register. In the baptismal register a loose sheet is inserted at the right date stating that this submersion has occurred.[1]

———————————————————————————————

The safeguards above duly protect the rite from being misunderstood as baptism—even by any who would like it to be. It totally entrenches the full sacramental standing of infant baptism already given in the candidates' lives. And even if, in any particular case, one or two safeguards were missing (as, for instance, if the preacher made little or no reference to the distinction between baptism and renewal, or if there were no actual baptismal candidates), yet the event would still be impregnably safeguarded by the other six or seven factors above.

[1] Where a candidate from one parish is thus submerged in another parish (as, e.g., when the two are grouped for confirmation purposes), then it is best if a loose sheet is clipped into *both* baptismal registers.

APPENDIX 1: THE RIGHT TERMS FOR THE DISCUSSION OF MODE

Whether we discuss baptism itself or rites for re-affirmation, we need to be clear about terminology. Thus, for instance, the House of Bishops' findings of November 1987 use 'immersion' to mean 'standing, sitting or kneeling in a baptistery in some water whilst other water is thrown or poured over the candidate'.[1] Many others, including standard dictionaries and some Baptists, use 'immersion' to mean 'total dunking', the very meaning from which the House of Bishops was trying to distinguish 'immersion'! I have worked hard myself to popularize 'submersion' for the 'total dunking'.[2] I now suggest that we need a five-tiered scale of terminology to communicate to each other aright:

1. Smearing: using a wet finger (not recommended, and arguably insufficient for baptism—the water should surely leave the hand?)

2. Sprinkling: separate drops reaching the candidate from the officiant (less than the Church of England's rubrics require for baptism, though possible for asperging)

3. Pouring: also called affusion, a continuous flow of water (even if only for a short time) reaching the candidate (the minimum required for baptism in the Church of England).

4. Placing in water with affusion: this is the difficult one to label—both 'dipping' and 'immersion' include both this and the next category, unless they are distinguished by adjectives ('total immersion' and 'less-than-total immersion'!). We need the language at least for debating purposes(!)—for it is not clear that the demand for the practice is high, save where ultra-purists have been engaged in salesmanship.

5. Submersion: going right under.

The Church of England rubrics have always included 'dip' as the first alternative (pouring being the second)—but the hint that the dipping is to be done 'warily' (which is quite otiose as a warning if it were category 4 under discussion) suggests strongly that it is category 5 which is intended. The advent of the theorists' position as category 4 has muddled the use of language, and 'dipping' and 'immersion' should not now be used without qualification.[3]

[1] See pages 17 above and 26 below.
[2] Totally clear terminology is found in J. G. Davies' book, *The Architectural Setting of Baptism* (Barrie and Rockcliff, 1962). His own descriptions of early church practice include (on pp.25-26) 'submersion', 'affusion' and 'standing in water and having his head dipped/immersed'.
[3] Most useful discussion, as has been shown, can be conducted by a simple adherence to the category 5 word 'submersion' (and a contrasting it with the category 3 word 'affusion'); category 4 still requires a long periphrasis, but, if it enters sufficiently into discussion in that shape, then some new clear term might be sought for it. But not, not, *not* 'immersion' *simpliciter*. The Toronto Statement (see footnote 3 on p.14 above) was very unhelpful at this point. Equally, Baptists and their ilk must be gently encouraged not to use unqualified 'immersion' for category 5, but to go over to 'submersion' for it. The New Zealand Presbyterian rite which follows in the next Appendix uses 'immersion' for category 5 innocently, but in the light of subsequent events, very unhelpfully.

APPENDIX 2: PART OF THE ARTICLE IN *THEOLOGICAL RENEWAL* **(1978)**
(The following extract is paragraph 6 in a much longer article)

— — — — — — — —

A rite of renewal
For the past five years the Doctrine Committee of the Presbyterian Church of New Zealand has been examining these issues and feeling its way toward providng a rite of 'renewal' which uses immersion.

In the outline liturgy which follows[1], the reader is asked to note carefully the meaning which has been built into the rite. From its use of scripture, statement of intention, prayers and words used at the moment of immersion, plainly this rite of renewal assumes baptism to be its antecedent. It reinforces the covenant meaning and relationship of baptism; it gives the candidates for immersion and the whole congregation an opportunity to join in a significant worshipful act of renewal and dedication.

ORDER OF WORSHIP

RITE OF RENEWAL

Introduction
Our help comes from the Lord who made heaven and earth.

We declare one Lord, one faith, one baptism, one God and Father of all who is over all, and through all and in all . . .' Each of us has been given his gift, his due portion of Christ's bounty, *(Eph. 4)*.

We declare that 'to us who are on the way to salvation the Cross of Jesus is the power of God' *(1 Cor. 1)*.

We declare that 'we were all brought into one body by baptism in the one Spirit . . . and that one Holy Spirit was poured out for us all to drink' *(1 Cor. 12)*.

'With all these witnesses to faith around us like a cloud we must throw off every incumbrance, every sin to which we cling, and run with resolution the race for which we are entered, our eyes fixed on Jesus on whom faith depends from start to finish.' *(Heb. 12)*.

Address Brothers and Sisters in Jesus Christ. In former days, before you knew it, God called you and laid his hand on you to be his. By your baptism you were ingrafted into the true Vine, who is Christ; incorporated into the body of Christ; seen to be infant members of the household of faith, lambs of the Good Shepherd's fold, to be nurtured in his grace.

Now by God's good hand, he has brought you here, personally to accept his grace and declare yourselves by the power of his Spirit to be his own in repentance, faith and service. From first to last this has been the work of God. 'He has reconciled us men to himself through Christ and has enlisted us in this service on reconciliation' (2 Cor. 5).

'So now, my friends, the sacrifice of Jesus makes us free to enter boldly into the sanctuary by the new and living way which he has opened for us . . . so let us make our approach with a sincere heart and a sure faith, with hearts made clean and bodies washed with pure water. Let us be firm and unswerving in the confession of our hope for the Giver of the promise may be trusted' (Heb. 10).

Prayer

Vows

Q1: Do you confess your faith in God as your Heavenly Father, in Jesus Christ as your Saviour and Lord, and in the Holy Spirit as your Sanctifier, Helper and Guide?

A: I do, with all my heart.

Q2: Do you sincerely repent of all your sin? Do you confess your need of Jesus, his cleansing and grace; and do you rely on his Holy Spirit to make you holy in God's sight?

A: I do repent; I submit to God's mercy in Jesus Christ; I give myself to him for his Spirit to fashion according to his will.

[1] This service was authorized by the General Assembly of the Presbyterian Church in New Zealand in November 1977 for use in congregations.

Q3: Do you promise, depending upon divine grace, to serve the Lord and to walk in his ways all the days of your life?'

A: I give myself to Jesus to follow him daily and serve him as Lord.

Q4: Do you promise to continue faithfully in the life, worship, witness and work of Christ's Church, using the gifts of grace which God by his Spirit gives you for his useful purpose?

A: I shall try so to live and work with all God's people for his praise and glory.

Q5: Do you submit to this act of immersion to show that you have put off the old man and have been buried with Christ in his death; and to show that you are now alive with Christ in the power of his resurrection, as he clothes you with his life and Spirit?'

A: With Paul the Apostle and all Christians I confess that 'the life I now live is not my life, but the life which Christ lives in me . . . Who loved me and gave himself for me'.

The Act

The officiating minister now immerses the candidates with the appropriate words— e.g.

As you were baptized in the name of the Father and of the Son and of the Holy Spirit, so now I confirm to you the cleansing, forgiveness, new life and promised gift of God's Spirit which are in his covenant.

or

As into Jesus Christ you were baptized, so I pray God who began a good work in you, to bring it to completion at the day of Christ Jesus.

The people's response and dedication

The Aaronic Blessing is sung by the Congregation.

Hymn (Those immersed change, or are wrapped warmly.)

Prayer (The congregation is invited to join in the following prayer, or similar prayers, preferably to be said in unison.)

Glorious and gracious God, we give you thanks for your grace and mercy in Jesus for all men.

We praise you this day for these, your servants, whom you called and claimed as your own.

As they have now confessed you, Lord Jesus, receive them.

We seek and claim the promise of your Holy Spirit upon them and us as one body in Jesus Christ.

May we all grow in grace, love and service, as true children and heirs of your covenant, for the upbuilding of the body of Christ, the salvation of men, and the coming of your Kingdom.

In joy, we cry 'Abba, Father' as your Spirit joins with our spirit to show that we are Christ's fellow-heirs. Help us, that if we must share in his suffering now, so also we shall share in his splendour hereafter. Keep us faithful, through Jesus Christ, our Lord. Amen.

The congregation confesses the faith in the words of the Creed.

Doxology (sung).

APPENDIX 3—COMMENT ON THE HOUSE OF BISHOPS' AGREED FINDINGS

(The text of the House of Bishops' minute of 21 October 1987 is to be found on page 17 above. In *News of Liturgy*, which I edit, for November 1987, I wrote an extended editorial on the minute. I reproduce it here without further editing.)

This is a mighty set of findings by the House of Bishops. As I want to comment especially upon the renewal of baptismal vows, I must not comment too freely on everything else. However the last paragraph tempts me out of my corner. It seems clear now that the House of Bishops is using immersion to mean 'standing in water, which is then poured over the candidate' and 'submersion' to mean 'dunking'. If this is the case, then one must point out:

(a)   This is a private linguistic use of the House—all Baptists and Brethren have always called dunking 'immersion' (and it is possible that I must myself bear some responsibility for popularizing the word 'submersion' in liturgical language, as I have steadfastly rejected the word 'immersion' for a word which means the *same* but has more popular usage). (We all know what an 'immersion heater' is—and it is right in and under the water . . .) In disavowing the use of 'immersion' I was never expecting it to crop up used in some different sense, as a variant on affusion, and thus distinguishable from 'dunking'.

(b)   The bishops treat 'dunking' as a 'present preferred option'. They seem to be ignorant of the fact that it is the first prescribed alternative in the rubrics of the BCP and the ASB. It is not a bright private idea someone has had—it is the official use of the Church of England passed by the House of Bishops (among others) less than ten years ago. If I understand aright what the House of Bishops means by 'immersion' (on which see (a) above), then it must be stated that it is without mention in the rubrics, without provision in Anglican baptismal architecture, and without much point either in relation to the stated need.

(c)   I am astonished to find that the House of Bishops knows what 'earliest Christian practice' was. So I hope they are not going to branch out into the public arena armed with esoteric information to which the rest of us do not have access. Let us take 'earliest' seriously—then the House of Bishops knows what apostolic practice was. (What there is, of course, is a likely fourth century and subsequent practice in which candidates stood in water and water was poured over them, or, possibly, they immersed their heads—but 'earliest', no . . .)

(d)   The practice recommended does not meet the pastoral need. Those who want to be submerged want to be submerged, and are unlikely to be amenable to unproven assertions about 'earliest Christian practice'. The impulse towards submersion is threefold—firstly, the death, burial, and resurrection *motif* of Romans 6; secondly, the desire for a total swamping as an experienced symbol of total commitment; and thirdly, the desire for a baptism recognizable and respected by those being baptized as adults in the Baptist, Brethren, and Pentecostalist denominations. This is where the pastoral need is. Who will say that the three aspects of the desire are so ungodly that candidates should be argued out of them? On the contrary, I would still maintain that the provisions of the rubric mean that all adults coming to baptism ought to be shown the rubrics, and be offered a choice of submersion or affusion. Candidates may well not want submersion, but, where they do, they respond to the first option in the rubrics. Who are the pastors who are to argue them out of it? the pastor's task is rather to find ways of providing it . . . (And it is the ultimate logic of 'a plentiful use of water', surely?)

Having got that out of my system, I pick up the renewal of baptismal vows. Apparently the House of Bishops is fearful lest such a rite may imply a renewal of baptism itself ((c) (iii)). It is not clear what error is thus excluded by their statement, but perhaps the House fears lest to 'renew' one's baptism is the same as 're-iterating' it. That would not be my view, and I have used the phrase 'renewal of your baptism' at some renewal of baptismal vows events, without any possibility that it could be mis-understood. However, once I knew that some folk distrusted the phrase, I changed it, and I now say on such occasions: 'NN, as you have been baptized in the name of the Father and of the Son and of the Holy Spirit, so now I dip you in this water in commemoration of that baptism and in renewal of its meaning for you, in the name of the Father and of the Son and of the Holy Spirit'. This is a slight change from the formula in Booklet no. 91, but perhaps prudent if 'renewal of baptism' is thought to produce a theological headache.

Thus, on the House of Bishops understanding, I join that House of Bishops in deprecating practices which appear to be a 'renewal of baptism'. If they think 'renewal' means 'repetition', I am with them. In my view, water can only be used at the renewal of baptismal vows with careful safeguards. I suggest the following:

(i) There must be careful preparation of candidates, so that they acknowledge they are already baptized.

(ii) There must be careful explanation in the preaching.

(iii) There must be careful distinguishing between baptism and the renewal of baptismal vows in the liturgical presentation (and my formula above is an instance of this—and certainly any such renewal of vows must not be physically mixed up with actual baptisms).

(iv) There should be proper documentation—including a certificate for each candidate, carrying the date and place of original baptism, and those of renewal of baptismal vows. I endeavour to get a loose page added to the baptismal register also, held by a paper-clip, and thus, without disturbing the baptismal register itself, giving evidence as to the rite used.

THE RENEWAL OF BAPTISMAL VOWS

So, if the Liturgical Commission is to prepare a 'more significant and dramatic rite' for the renewal of baptismal vows, they could do much worse than look at the use of submersion.

This is where the pastoral need is, and the minutes of the House do not touch on that point. There are many who were baptized as infants who would now readily leave the Church of England and have baptism *ab initio*. Some of them can be contained by submersion with renewal of vows. A rationale is ready to hand for this. It would be astonishing if the Church of England were ready to be flexible to the point of abolishing all principles when admitting to baptism the infants of non-worshippers—but is wholly unready to be flexible towards the tender conscience of some of her own best children, when meeting that tenderness involves no surrender of principles at all. I say 'it would be', but fortunately that is not the case. On what I think to be the Bishops' understanding of 'renewal of baptism' I too would abjure it. A charitable reading of the minute of the House would suggest they are tacitly in favour of the practices I have described as my own, and that is a relief.

28